# FOOD LOVERS

# SOUP

## RECIPES SELECTED BY ALEKSANDRA MALYSKA

Trans
Atlantic
Press

# All recipes serve four people, unless otherwise indicated.

For best results when cooking the recipes in this book, buy fresh ingredients and follow the instructions carefully. Make sure that everything is properly cooked through before serving, particularly any meat and shellfish, and note that as a general rule vulnerable groups such as the very young, elderly people, pregnant women, convalescents and anyone suffering from an illness should avoid dishes that contain raw or lightly cooked eggs.

For all recipes, quantities are given in standard U.S. cups and imperial measures, followed by the metric equivalent. Follow one set or the other, but not a mixture of both because conversions may not be exact. Standard spoon and cup measurements are level and are based on the following:

1 tsp. = 5 ml, 1 tbsp. = 15 ml, 1 cup = 250 ml / 8 fl oz.

Note that Australian standard tablespoons are 20 ml, so Australian readers should use 3 tsp. in place of 1 tbsp. when measuring small quantities.

The electric oven temperatures in this book are given for conventional ovens with top and bottom heat. When using a fan oven, the temperature should be decreased by about 20–40ºF / 10–20ºC – check the oven manufacturer's instruction book for further guidance. The cooking times given should be used as an approximate guideline only.

# CONTENTS

# CHILLED TOMATO SOUP WITH CROÛTONS

## Ingredients

2¼ lb /1 kg tomatoes

1 onion

3 cloves garlic

1 bunch parsley

1 bunch basil

2 sprigs thyme

1 sprig savory

2 tbsp. olive oil

Salt & freshly milled pepper

2 slices rye bread

3 tbsp. butter, to fry

## Method

Prep and cook time: 1 h plus 1 h refrigeration time

**1** Quarter and deseed the tomatoes. Peel and quarter the onion and garlic.

**2** Put the tomatoes into a blender with the chopped herbs, onion, garlic and salt and blend.

**3** Push through a sieve if you wish. Season to taste with salt and pepper.

**4** Stir in the olive oil and chill in the refrigerator for at least an hour.

**5** Dice the bread, fry in butter and scatter over the soup before serving.

# SWEET POTATO SOUP WITH LENTILS AND BALSAMIC ONIONS

## Ingredients

1 onion

1 lb 2 oz /450 g sweet potatoes

1 leek

½ cup /100 g red lentils

2 tbsp. /25 g butter

1 clove garlic

1 tsp. ground coriander

4 cups /500 ml vegetable broth (stock)

Salt & freshly milled pepper

2 tbsp. snipped chives

In addition:

2 red onions

1 tbsp. butter

4 tbsp. balsamic vinegar

Balsamic onions, to garnish

## Method

Prep and cook time: 1 h

**1** Peel and finely dice the onion. Peel and chop the sweet potatoes. Trim and slice the leek. Wash the lentils under running water.

**2** Heat the butter and sauté the onion until translucent, press in the garlic and sauté briefly. Stir in the coriander, then add the sweet potatoes and leek and sauté, stirring, for about 5 minutes.

**3** Add the vegetable broth (stock) and the lentils, cover and simmer for about 30 minutes.

**4** Meanwhile peel and slice the red onions and sauté in butter until soft. Add the balsamic vinegar and simmer until slightly reduced.

**5** Remove the soup from the heat, season to taste with salt and pepper, stir in the chives and ladle into plates or bowls. Serve garnished with balsamic onions.

# TAMARIND AND COCONUT SOUP

## Ingredients

⅓ cup /80 ml sesame oil

1 red onion, peeled and chopped

2 cloves garlic, peeled and chopped

1 red chili, chopped

1–2 tsp. cumin

1 tsp. ground coriander

2 very ripe plantains, peeled and cut into ½ inch (1 cm) slices

2½ cups /600 ml chicken broth (stock)

¼ cup /50 ml tamarind paste

1¼ cups /300 ml unsweetened coconut milk

1 tsp. sea salt

½ cup roughly chopped cilantro (coriander) leaves

½ cup roughly chopped fresh mint leaves

## Method

Prep and cook time: 30 min

**1** Heat the sesame oil in a large pan and add the red onion, garlic, half of the chili, cumin and ground coriander. Sauté for 5 minutes, stirring continuously so it doesn't stick.

**2** Add the plantains, broth (stock), tamarind paste and coconut milk and bring to a boil. Turn the heat to a gentle simmer and cook until the plantains are soft, then remove from the heat.

**3** Add the salt and purée the soup. Return to the heat and add the rest of the chili.

**4** Stir in the cilantro (coriander) and mint just before serving.

# CREAMED PUMPKIN SOUP WITH GINGER AND STRIPS OF CHILI

## Ingredients

1 lb /500 g pumpkin, diced

1 onion

1 clove garlic

1 tsp. fresh ginger, chopped

2 tbsp. butter

3¼ cups /800 ml vegetable broth (stock)

¾–1 cup /200 ml light (single) cream

2 tbsp chopped walnuts

Salt

Cayenne pepper

Brown sugar

Chili threads, dried

## Method

Prep and cook time: 45 min

**1** Peel the pumpkin, remove the seeds and dice. Peel the onion and the garlic and finely chop.

**2** Sauté the pumpkin, onion, garlic and ginger in hot butter, then pour in the vegetable broth (stock) and cream. Simmer over a low heat for about 30 minutes.

**3** In the meantime roughly chop the walnuts and toast in a dry, hot skillet.

**4** Purée the soup, season with salt, cayenne pepper and sugar and spoon into 4 bowls. Garnish with the chopped walnuts and chili threads and serve.

# LENTIL SOUP WITH SAUSAGE AND LEEKS

## Ingredients

1 cup /150 g brown lentils

2 carrots

10 oz /300 g boiling potatoes

1 leek

1 onion

1 clove garlic

1 tbsp. oil

4 oz /100 g bacon cubes

2 cloves

1 bay leaf

6 cups /1½ litres beef broth (stock)

10 oz /300 g Bologna, Lyoner or Mortadella sausage

Salt & freshly milled pepper

2 tbsp. chopped fresh parsley, to garnish

## Method

Prep and cook time: 1 h  Soaking time: 12 h

**1** Rinse the lentils under cold water in a sieve. Place in a bowl, cover with fresh water and soak overnight. Drain well.

**2** Peel and dice the carrots and the potatoes. Trim the leek and cut into 2 inch (5 cm) long, thin strips. Chop the onion and finely mince the garlic.

**3** Heat the oil in a large pan and sauté the bacon, onions and garlic until soft. Add the carrots, potato and leek and sauté. Now throw in the bay leaf and the cloves, pour in the beef broth (stock) and add the lentils. Bring to a boil, then reduce the heat and simmer for about 45 minutes. Remove the bay leaf and the cloves. Process about one third of the soup in a blender until smooth. Pour back into the pan.

**4** Peel the skin off the sausage and cut into thin rings. Place in the soup and simmer for 5 minutes. Season with salt and pepper. Serve in bowls and garnish with the chopped parsley.

# GARLIC SOUP WITH BREAD

## Ingredients

12 cloves garlic, plus some to garnish

4 cups /1 litre vegetable broth (stock)

2 tbsp. olive oil

2 bay leaves

1 sprig sage

1 cup /100 g grated Parmesan cheese

2 egg yolks

2 tbsp. whipping cream

Salt & freshly milled pepper

2 tbsp. sherry

1 tbsp. lemon juice

1 tbsp. mustard

4 toasted baguette slices

Fresh parsley, to garnish

## Method

Prep and cook time: 30 min

**1** Peel the garlic and put it into a pan with the vegetable broth (stock), olive oil, bay and sage leaves and bring to a boil. Simmer, half-covered with a lid, for 15 minutes.

**2** Take out the bay leaves and sage and purée the soup with a hand blender.

**3** Mix the Parmesan cheese, egg yolks and cream.

**4** Remove the soup from the heat and carefully stir in the cheese mixture. Season with salt and pepper and add sherry, lemon juice and mustard to taste.

**5** Ladle the soup into 4 soup bowls and add a toasted baguette slice to each. Serve garnished with garlic and parsley.

# FISH SOUP WITH POTATOES

## Ingredients

2 tbsp. olive oil

2 onions, finely chopped

2 cloves garlic, finely chopped

1–2 small red chilies, de-seeded and finely chopped

1 packet saffron threads

14 oz /400 g chopped canned tomatoes

1 tbsp. tomato paste (purée)

¾–1 cup /200 ml white wine

14 oz /400 g small whole potatoes, for boiling

Salt & freshly milled pepper

12 oz /350 g mixed seafood, such as mussels, clams, shrimps, squid

1 lb 6 oz /600 g fish fillets, such as cod, perch, tuna

½ bunch fresh parsley, chopped

## Method

Prep and cook time: 1 h

**1** Heat the olive oil in a large skillet. Fry the onions, garlic, chili and saffron threads over a medium heat for about 10 minutes.

**2** Add the tomatoes, tomato paste (purée) and pour in the white wine. Bring to a boil, then reduce the heat and simmer for 5 minutes.

**3** Peel the potatoes and dice if necessary, and then add to the pan and simmer gently for 15 minutes. Season with salt and pepper.

**4** Clean the seafood and add to the soup. Place the fish fillets on the top. Cover and simmer for a further 10 minutes over a medium heat.

**5** Spoon into 4 bowls, sprinkle with freshly chopped parsley and serve.

# FRENCH ONION SOUP WITH CHEESE BAGUETTES

## Ingredients

For the soup:

3¼ lbs /1½ kg onions

4 oz / 100 g butter

4 cups /1 litre vegetable broth (stock)

1 cup /240 ml dry white wine

Pinch nutmeg

1 tsp. fresh or ½ tsp. dried thyme

Pinch ground caraway

Salt & freshly milled pepper


For the garnish:

4–8 slices baguette

2 cloves garlic, peeled

2 oz /50 g Gruyere cheese, grated

## Method
Prep and cook time: 45 min

**1** Peel the onions and finely slice. Heat the butter in a large pan and fry the onions until soft. Pour in the vegetable broth (stock) and the wine and season with nutmeg, thyme and ground caraway. Bring to a boil, and then simmer for 25–30 minutes.

**2** Toast the slices of baguette and rub a peeled garlic clove over the top of the baguette, then use a garlic press to crush the rest of the garlic into the soup.

**3** Season the soup with salt and pepper and spoon into 4 ovenproof bowls. Arrange the baguette slices on top of the soup, sprinkle the grated cheese over the top and place under the broiler (grill) for a few minutes until the cheese has melted.

**4** Sprinkle with freshly ground black pepper and serve immediately.

# KALE AND SPINACH SOUP

## Ingredients

2 tbsp. oil

1 clove garlic, finely diced

1 onion, finely diced

1½ oz /40 g smoked bacon, roughly diced

10 oz /300 g kale, shredded

4 oz /100 g spinach, shredded

4 oz /100 g kohlrabi, sliced (or turnip if not available)

3 oz /75 g carrots, diced

7 oz /200 g baking potatoes, diced

Scant ½ cup /100 ml white wine

3¼ cups /800 ml vegetable broth (stock)

1 tsp. lemon juice

Salt & freshly milled pepper


For the garnish:

4 oz /100 g white sandwich bread, diced

1 oz /25 g butter

2 tbsp. crème fraîche

Grated Parmesan cheese

## Method

Prep and cook time: 50 min

**1**  Heat the oil in a large pan and sauté the onions, garlic and bacon, stirring continually. Add the rest of the vegetables and sauté for a few minutes.

**2**  Pour in the white wine and the vegetable broth (stock). Bring to a boil, and then simmer over a low heat for about 20 minutes.

**3**  Take about ⅓ of the vegetables out of the pot and put on the side. Finely purée the soup and season to taste with salt, pepper and lemon juice. Put the vegetables back into the soup and warm.

**4**  Cut the crusts off the white sandwich bread and cut into small cubes. Melt the butter in a skillet and toss the croutons in the butter until golden brown. Take out of the skillet and season with salt.

**5**  Spoon the soup into 4 soup bowls, put a few croutons over the top. Add a spoonful of crème fraîche and serve with a sprinkle of grated Parmesan cheese.

# HERB SOUP WITH CROÛTONS

## Ingredients

4 oz /100 g spinach

1–2 shallot

4 oz /100 g potatoes

2 tbsp. butter

3 cups /700 ml chicken broth (stock)

Scant ½ cup /100 g whipping cream)

2 tbsp. crème fraîche

1–2 handfuls mixed herbs (chervil,
parsley, basil, sorrel)

Salt & freshly milled pepper


To garnish:

2 slices white bread

2 tbsp. butter

Bunch fresh parsley

## Method
Prep and cook time: 40 min

**1** Wash the spinach and blanch in boiling, salted
water for a few minutes. Refresh in cold water, drain
well, and then chop.

**2** Peel and finely chop the shallots. Peel and finely
grate the potatoes.

**3** Sauté the shallots in hot butter until soft. Pour
in the chicken broth (stock) and add the potatoes.
Simmer for about 10 minutes. Now pour in the
cream and crème fraîche and add the spinach and
herbs. Bring to a boil, then purée until smooth.

**4** Cut the crusts off the bread and chop into cubes.
Fry the bread in hot butter until golden brown.

**5** Season the soup to taste with salt and pepper
and serve with a few croûtons and a few sprigs of
parsley.

# RED LENTIL SOUP

## Ingredients

1 lb /450g pack of soup vegetables; carrot, celery root (celeriac), leek

2 cups /400 g red lentils

4 cups / 1 litre beef broth (stock)

1 bay leaf

1 tsp. dried thyme

2 tsp. lemon zest, grated

1 tbsp. tomato concentrate

3 tbsp. balsamic vinegar

Salt & freshly milled pepper

Pinch sugar


For the garnish:

2 slices wholemeal bread

2 tbsp. butter

Fresh basil leaves, shredded

## Method
Prep and cook time: 40 min

**1** Finely chop the soup vegetables. Wash the lentils in a sieve under cold, running water, then place in the beef broth (stock) and bring to a boil.

**2** Add the chopped vegetables, the bay leaf and the thyme and simmer for about 20 minutes. As soon as the lentils are soft, remove the bay leaf and purée the soup.

**3** Cut the crusts off the bread, cut the bread into cubes and fry in the butter until golden brown. Set aside.

**4** Put the grated lemon zest and tomato concentrate in the soup, cover with a lid and warm through. Season with balsamic vinegar, salt, pepper and a pinch of sugar. Serve in warmed bowls, sprinkle a few croutons over the top and garnish with shredded basil leaves.

# BROCCOLI SOUP WITH CORN KERNELS AND MUSHROOMS

## Ingredients

1 onion

3 cloves garlic

1 head of broccoli

7 oz /200 g button mushrooms

10 oz /280 g can of corn kernels

3 tbsp. butter

3¼ cups / 800 ml vegetable broth (stock)

1 tbsp. flour

Scant ½ cup / 100 g whipping cream

Salt & freshly milled pepper

1 tbsp. finely chopped parsley leaves

## Method

Prep and cook time: 40 min

**1** Peel and finely chop the onion and garlic. Divide the broccoli into small florets. Clean the mushrooms and cut into smaller pieces if necessary. Drain the corn kernels.

**2** Heat 2 tablespoons of the butter in a pan and sauté the onion and garlic until translucent. Add the mushrooms and broccoli and sauté all together. Pour in the broth (stock) and bring to a boil. Reduce the heat, cover and simmer for 15 minutes.

**3** Blend together the remaining butter and the flour and stir the paste into the soup. Stir in the cream and corn kernels and briefly bring to a boil.

**4** Season with salt and pepper

# CREAMY BLUE CHEESE SOUP

## Ingredients

1 onion

1 potato

1 lb / 450 g celery root (celeriac)

2 tbsp butter

3 cups / 750 ml chicken or vegetable broth (stock)

3 oz / 75 g blue cheese

1 cup / 250 ml whipping cream

Celery leaves or parsley, to garnish

## Method

Prep and cook time: 30 min

**1** Chop the onion finely. Peel and dice the potato. Peel and chop the celery root (celeriac). Heat the butter in a large pan and gently cook the onion until soft but not brown.

**2** Add the potato and celeriac, cook for 2 minutes then pour in the broth (stock). Bring to a boil then simmer gently for 20 minutes or until the vegetables are very soft. Add the cheese and stir until the cheese has melted.

**3** Add the cream to the soup, reserving a little for garnish. Blend to a smooth purée then pass through a fine sieve into a clean pan. Reheat gently, season with salt and pepper and serve garnished with a swirl of cream and the celery leaves or parsley.

# SPICY CORN CREAM SOUP WITH FRIED BACON

## Ingredients

1 onion

1 red chili

2 tbsp butter

2 tbsp flour

3 cups / 750 ml vegetable broth (stock)

10 oz / 280 g canned sweetcorn, drained

½ cup / 125 ml whipping cream

2 slices bacon, fried till crisp

Parsley, to garnish

## Method

Prep and cook time: 30 min

**1** Finely chop the onion. De-seed and finely chop the chili. Heat the butter in a large pan and gently cook the onion until soft. Reserve a little of the chopped chili for the garnish and add the rest to the pan.

**2** Sprinkle the flour into the pan, cook for 1 minute, stirring all the time, then gradually add the vegetable broth (stock).

**3** Bring to a boil then simmer gently for 10 minutes. Reserve about a quarter of the sweetcorn and add the remainder to the pan. Blend the soup until smooth then pass through a fine sieve into a clean pan.

**4** Stir in the cream and the remaining sweetcorn, reheat gently and season with salt and pepper. Serve the soup in warmed bowls garnished with the remaining red chili, the crumbled bacon and the parsley.

# HOT AND SOUR SHRIMP SOUP

## Ingredients

4 oz /125 g straw mushrooms, enoki or white mushrooms

1 stalk lemongrass

5 hot green Thai chilies

2 cloves garlic

3 cups /700 ml chicken broth (stock)

3 kaffir lime leaves

2 slices fresh galangal, if available

1–2 tbsp. fish sauce

7 oz /200 g shrimps (or prawns), cleaned and shelled

1–2 tbsp. lime juice

A few cilantro (coriander) leaves, to garnish

## Method

Prep and cook time: 20 min

**1** Clean and slice the mushrooms. Cut the lemongrass stalk into about 1 inch (3 cm) lengths. Slice the chilies diagonally. Chop the garlic.

**2** Pour the chicken broth (stock) into a saucepan and bring to a boil, then reduce the heat. Add the mushrooms, lemongrass, chilies, garlic, lime leaves, galangal and 1 tablespoon of fish sauce and simmer for about 4 minutes. Add the shrimps and cook very gently for about 1 minute.

**3** Remove the lemongrass from the soup. Season to taste with fish sauce and lime juice and serve garnished with cilantro (coriander) leaves.

# CARROT AND ORANGE SOUP

## Ingredients

2 tbsp. butter

1 onion, chopped

6 carrots, peeled and grated

1 potato, baking, peeled and grated

2½ cups /600 ml vegetable broth (stock)

2 oranges, grated zest and juice

2 tbsp. crème fraîche

Pinch cayenne pepper

2 tbsp. fresh parsley, chopped

Salt & freshly milled pepper

## Method

Prep and cook time: 30 min

**1** Sauté the chopped onion in hot butter, add the grated carrots and potato, season with salt, cover and cook for about 5 minutes.

**2** Now pour in enough vegetable broth (stock) so that the vegetables are covered. Add the orange zest, cover and simmer for a further 10 minutes.

**3** Purée the soup until smooth. Add the orange juice and the crème fraîche and stir. Pour in a little vegetable broth, depending on the thickness of the soup.

**4** Season to taste with salt and cayenne pepper. Garnish with chopped parsley and freshly milled pepper and serve.

# TOMATO AND BEET SOUP WITH FETA CHEESE

## Ingredients

14 oz /400 g beet (beetroot)

3 cups /750 ml vegetable broth (stock)

7 oz / 200 g chopped tomatoes (canned)

Salt & freshly milled pepper

Juice of ½ lemon

4 oz / 100 g feta cheese, diced

Oregano, to garnish

## Method

Prep and cook time: 30 min  Chilling time: 2 h

**1** Peel and dice the beet (beetroot) and simmer in the vegetable broth (stock) over a low heat for about 15 minutes.

**2** Then add the tomatoes and simmer for a further 5 minutes. Blend in a blender.

**3** Now either leave the soup to go cold and season to taste, or serve hot.

**4** To serve hot, return to a boil, season with salt and pepper and add lemon juice to taste.

**5** Put a little feta cheese in each bowl and ladle the soup over it (hot or cold). Serve garnished with oregano.

# ANDALUSIAN FISH SOUP WITH CHILIES

## Ingredients

1 lb 2 oz /500 g monkfish fillets, or sea bream

1 onion

2 cloves garlic

1 chili

1 sprig rosemary

4 tbsp. olive oil

4 tomatoes

2 yellow bell peppers

½ bunch basil

4 sprigs thyme

1¾ cups /400 ml tomato juice

¾–1 cup / 200 ml fish broth (stock)

Salt & freshly milled pepper

Tabasco sauce

## Method

Prep and cook time: 25 min plus 2 h marinating time

**1** Cut the fish into bite-size pieces. Peel the onion and the garlic, finely chop the garlic and roughly chop the onion. Slice the chili into thin rings.

**2** Finely chop the rosemary leaves. Mix with the oil, chili, garlic and fish and leave for about 2 hours to marinate.

**3** Chop the tomatoes. Halve, de-seed and chop the bell peppers. Finely chop the basil and thyme leaves, saving some for the garnish.

**4** Take the fish out of the marinade and fry in a skillet until golden brown, then remove. Heat the marinade in a large pan and sauté the onion. Add the bell peppers, the tomatoes and pour in the tomato juice and the fish broth (stock). Simmer gently for about 10 minutes. Mix in the chopped herbs and season to taste with salt, pepper and Tabasco sauce.

**5** Place the fish in the soup, warm through and serve.

# TYROLEAN BARLEY SOUP WITH SMOKED PORK AND VEGETABLES

## Ingredients

½ cup /100 g barley

1 onion

2 oz /50 g streaky bacon, diced

Salt & freshly milled pepper

Pinch nutmeg

3 cups /700 ml beef broth (stock)

7 oz /200 g smoked cured pork, without the bone, pre-cooked

8 oz / 250 g pumpkin

1 leek

2 stalks celery

A few celery leaves, to garnish

## Method

Prep and cook time: 1 h

**1** Wash the barley and drain well. Peel and finely chop the onion. Dice the bacon and fry in a skillet, without fat. Add the barley and the onions and sauté. Season with salt, pepper and nutmeg and pour in the beef broth (stock). Bring to a boil, and then simmer for 20–25 minutes.

**2** In the meantime, cut the pork into 1-inch (2–3 cm) cubes. Dice the pumpkin, cut the leek into thin rings, slice the celery thinly. Put the pork and the vegetables in the soup and cook until soft.

**3** Season the soup to taste, garnish with a few celery leaves and serve.

# SPICY PEA AND VEGETABLE SOUP

## Ingredients

$^2/_3$ cup / 100 g brown dried peas

Olive oil

1 tsp. cumin seed

3 cloves garlic, finely chopped

4 scallions (spring onions), chopped

2 tsp. grated ginger

2 tsp. garam masala

2–3 green chillies, deseeded and finely chopped

14 oz/ 400 g cauliflower, divided into small florets

14 oz / 400 g pumpkin, diced

3 cups / 750 ml water

1 tsp. tomato purée

Salt

1–2 tbsp. sour cream, to garnish

## Method

Prep and cook time: 1 h  Soaking time: 12 h

**1** Soak the peas in water overnight.

**2** Drain and rinse the peas. Heat 4–5 tablespoons of oil in a wide pan and briefly sauté the cumin seeds. Add the garlic, scallions (spring onions), ginger, garam masala and chili and sauté briefly.

**3** Add the pumpkin and cauliflower, sauté briefly, then add the water. Stir in the tomato purée and peas, season with 1–2 teaspoons of salt and bring to a boil. Then reduce the heat, cover and simmer over a low heat for 30–35 minutes.

**4** Season to taste with salt. Ladle into soup bowls and serve. Add 1–2 tablespoons sour cream to each bowl, if desired.

# PEA SOUP WITH CRÈME FRAÎCHE

## Ingredients

1 shallot

1 clove garlic

1 tbsp. butter

$2^2/_3$ cups /400 g frozen peas

1 tsp. ginger, freshly grated

$2^1/_2$ cups /600 ml chicken broth (stock)

Scant ½ cup /100 ml whipping cream

Salt & freshly milled pepper

2 tbsp. crème fraîche

## Method

Prep and cook time: 20 min

**1** Peel and finely chop the shallot and garlic. Heat the butter and sauté the shallot and garlic, then add the peas and ginger. Pour in the chicken broth (stock) and bring to a boil.

**2** Simmer the soup for 6–8 minutes, then add the cream and purée the soup finely. Push through a sieve if you wish.

**3** Season to taste with salt and pepper and ladle into bowls. Add a swirl of crème fraîche to each and serve.

# BUTTERNUT SQUASH SOUP

## Ingredients

1 onion

1 clove garlic

1 tsp. ginger, finely grated

1 red chili

1 lb 12 oz /800 g butternut squash

4 tbsp. oil

1 tbsp. sugar

2 cups /500 ml vegetable broth (stock)

Scant ½ cup /100 ml orange juice

¾–1 cup / 200 g whipping cream

Salt & freshly milled pepper

1 tsp. curry powder

Ground nutmeg

Thyme, to garnish

For the croutons:

2 slices white bread, from the previous day

2 tbsp. butter

## Method

Prep and cook time: 1 h

**1**   Peel and dice the onion and garlic. De-seed and finely chop the chili. Peel and deseed and dice the butternut squash.

**2**  Heat the oil in a pan and sauté the onion, garlic, ginger and chili and butternut squash. Sprinkle with sugar and stir over the heat until lightly caramelized. Now add the broth (stock), cover and cook gently for about 35 minutes, until soft.

**3**  Purée the soup. Add the orange juice and cream and bring to a boil. Season with salt and pepper and add curry powder and nutmeg to taste.

**4**  To make the croutons, cut the white bread into cubes and fry in butter until golden brown. Season with salt and pepper and drain on a paper towel.

**5**  Ladle the hot soup into bowls and serve garnished with thyme and croutons.

Published by Transatlantic Press

First published in 2010

Transatlantic Press
38 Copthorne Road, Croxley Green, Hertfordshire WD3 4AQ

© Transatlantic Press

Images and Recipes by StockFood © The Food Image Agency

Recipes selected by Aleksandra Malyska, StockFood

A catalogue record for this book is available from the British Library.

ISBN 978-1-908533-56-2

Printed in China